Praise for *Forgo*

"This is a splendid little book, offering insights on dreams, memory, and caregiving in a gentle and compassionate voice. Author Gover, a dream worker, teacher, and frequent presenter, anchors her book with personal anecdotes of her relationship with her mother as her mother struggled through Alzheimer's Disease. Gover encourages us to trust our dreams, including our nightmares, as occasions for healing. Two nuggets will stay with me for a long time: the idea that our dreams offer us emotional connection with the people we love when they can no longer talk with us; and our dreams can help us heal relationships and resolve personal issues. Written in simple language with short sections, this is a book that understands the challenges caregivers face and offers a bit of light for the journey."

Jeanne Van Bronkhorst, *Dreams at the Threshold: Guidance, Comfort, and Healing at the End of Life.*

"A rare glimpse into a mother-daughter bonding experience through dreams at a time when communication was all but lost to Alzheimer's disease. Not only that, but how to get more precious sleep during a time of insomnia and insanity. I'm comforted by this ebook. Highly recommend for those who are desperate to connect with a loved one afflicted by Alzheimer's."

Sharon Pastore, CDP, Founder, Dream Girl Power

Forgotten Dreams

Tapping into the Power of Sleep and Dreams for Caregivers of People with Dementia and Alzheimer's

by Tzivia Gover, author of *The Mindful Way to a Good Night's Sleep,* Certified Dreamwork Professional, and Director of the Institute for Dream Studies

Forgotten Dreams

Tapping into the Power of Sleep and Dreams for Caregivers of People with Dementia and Alzheimer's

Tzivia Gover

Third House Moon
PO Box 145
Northampton, Mass. 01061-0145

ISBN 9781796662672

Edited by Suzanne Wilson

Interior Design by Bridgette O'Hare, Dark Unicorn Designs

The information in this book is true and complete to the best of our knowledge. All recommendations are made without guarantee on the part of the author. The author disclaims any liability in connection with the use of this information.

Tzivia Gover's books are widely available. Visit **www.tziviagover.com** for more.

Dedication

I dedicate this book to my brother, James Gover, who has shown me how to give care with a full heart, and to my mother, Jane Covell, who was a beautiful dreamer.

෧

The Dream Hotel

I dream about a hotel.
It is big, rambling.
There are halls that do not lead anywhere.
There are no sounds.
There are elevators that do not work.
There are doors that do not open
Or the doors open to nightmares.
There are no windows in this hotel. It is always
dark.
I am lost; I am frightened.
I often dream about this hotel.

Jane Covell
1934-2015

Table of Contents

Author's Note

When my mother began to slip into dementia I became one of her caregivers, along with my brother and a handful of devoted paid professionals. Although I'm a self-help author whose job it is to coach others to take good care of themselves and seek support when appropriate, in this situation it was hard for me to find the time and money to attend to my own needs.

At times I felt angry and resentful, or I was depleted, often depressed, and despairing that my beautiful, intelligent, and loving mother was beset with such an insidious disease. And then, I felt abandoned and alone as I struggled with my physical and mental well-being in the face of my new role and responsibilities as my mother's caregiver—when I really only wanted to be her daughter, enjoying her friendship, laughter and love.

I was in good company. I met dozens of other family members at the memory care facility where my mother spent her final days and even more through participating in annual Alzheimer's Association walks and events. "We're all in the same boat," I'd say on meeting other caregivers. Then I'd add, "and it's a really big boat!" In fact, there are some 5.7 million people with Alzheimer's and related dementias in the United States plus over 16 million unpaid caregivers and a growing corps of paid caregivers attending to them.

Caring for the emotional and physical needs of a family member or other loved one with dementia isn't easy. The demands can mount slowly—from picking up groceries or monitoring finances to arranging for and overseeing medical care. Add to that the emotional confusion that sets in when an adult son or daughter takes on the parenting role for their mom or dad, or when a life partner becomes nurse and keeper for their significant other. Even under the best of circumstances, with financial resources and strong social networks, the responsibilities and emotional intensity add up. There's no question that the taxing nature of being a caregiver takes its toll on physical health and mental well-being.

In my case, caring for my mom included frequent commutes from my home in western Massachusetts to hers in New York City, as well as paying her bills, battling insurance companies' capricious denials of coverage, and coordinating paid caregivers from afar. To make matters more challenging, this new responsibility and the heartbreak that came with it began just after my relationship of nearly two decades ended, my daughter left home for college, and I was laid off from my job. Concerned friends suggested I attend one of a handful of support groups in my area for family members of people with Alzheimer's or dementia, but I simply couldn't fit in one more thing. Other self-care fixes, like getting a massage, taking long baths, or taking some extra "me" time likewise felt out of reach—either because of cost, time, or both.

But I did have one source of generous, wise guidance close at hand, and it was free of charge and required no extra time or travel. All my life I've had a strong connection with my nighttime dreams. And they didn't let me down during the 10 years that I accompanied my mother on her journey through Alzheimer's disease. My dreams coached me and comforted me, and thanks to them I found spiritual strength and meaning through what would otherwise have felt like a devastating ordeal.

In the pages that follow I will share my story about my experience with my mother and Alzheimer's, including some pivotal dreams and how I used them to help navigate the sometimes nightmarish terrain of loving someone with dementia. I will also draw on my professional expertise as a dreamworker who has worked with hundreds of clients, many of whom have been caregivers themselves, and as an author who has researched and written books on the topics of sleep, dreams and the practice and benefits of mindfulness. Drawing from this background, I will share tips, techniques, and resources for caregivers so they too can use the gifts of their nighttime dreams for support and guidance.

"Without forgetting it is quite impossible to live at all."

— Friedrich Nietzsche, *On the Advantage and Disadvantage of History for Life*

Dreams with Benefits

One night I dreamed I was in a foreign city, but I couldn't remember which one. Nor could I recall which airport I'd flown into, or why I was there. But then, I realized I was dreaming, and suddenly the city's name or how I arrived was no longer important.

I woke with a smile. After all, isn't the same true in waking life? When we remember that all of life is, as the song goes, "but a dream" it's easier to stop sweating the small stuff—and even some of the big stuff—and just go along for the ride.

Sleep has been called "The Land of Nod," but it can as easily be thought of as "The Land of Forgetting." In dreams we routinely forget who we are, who our partner or spouse is, and even where home is. In this nightly land of forgetting we can't spell simple words, usually can't even read. More often than not we can't dial a phone properly, and when we try to call for help, words fail us, as though we've lost our power of speech.

In sleep and dreams we enter a world that bears some resemblance to the realm inhabited by our loved ones with dementia. The big difference is that each morning we get to wake back up to our familiar minds with our memories and abilities intact.

Here are some of the benefits I have gleaned from sleep and dreams, and which I offer to you:

- Paying attention to dreams can help us practice moving from forgetfulness to memory with grace. An awareness of our dreams can also help us have increased empathy for our loved ones who live full time now in "The Land of Forgetting."

- Dreams provide a spiritual viewpoint. They can help caregivers make sense of their situation, offer uplift, and inspire them through difficult times.

- Dreams can help us feel connected to our loved ones. When we can no longer talk to them as we once did, due to cognitive issues or death, dreams offer a way to visit with them in ways that feel authentic.

Forgotten Dreams

- Through dreams and dreamwork we can resolve issues we thought were beyond reconciliation, as dreams can be a catalyst for healing.

Tzivia Gover

Sleep, Memory

A Dreamscape of Loss and Hope

In order to dream, first you need to sleep. And that isn't easy for caregivers, many of whom are beset by the unhappy bedfellows of fatigue and insomnia.

For those who live with—or sleep with—someone with Alzheimer's or dementia, getting a good night's rest can be challenging. People with dementia might wake from nightmares and be difficult to console so that they and their caregiver can return to sleep. Incontinence might also be an issue, leading to late-night cleanups and changes of bedding and pajamas.

Even for caregivers who live across town—or across the country— sleep can be interrupted by worrisome thoughts, anxiety or depression. Freed from the day-to-day tasks of the in-home caregiver, the caregiver living at a distance might feel helpless and even guilty at being so far away. Plus, troubling dreams might wake the caregiver, who may then be beset with disturbing images and feel too uneasy to sleep.

Whatever the reasons, settling the body and mind enough to enjoy a full eight hours of restorative sleep is often elusive. Making matters worse, we know that losing sleep adds to stress-related health issues.

Then there's the elephant in the middle of the (bed)room. Caregivers of those with memory issues may be genetically at greater risk of suffering cognitive issues of their own. On top of that, studies show that people who experience less than optimal time in REM sleep are more prone to developing Alzheimer's. We know that dreams and dreamwork help with problem solving, stress reduction, and physical and emotional healing—all benefits that are much needed by caregivers. But without sleep, we can't enter REM, where our most vivid and memorable dreams take place.

So those with a loved one who has Alzheimer's disease or other forms of dementia, while keyed in to the importance of a good night's rest, grow anxious about their lack of sleep and what it might be doing to their own chances of having severe memory issues down the line. These anxieties don't make getting to sleep any easier. And so we have a vicious cycle: One of the functions of sleep and dreams is to help consolidate and organize memory, and yet staying up nights worrying about our cognitive health only makes things worse.

To try to interrupt this cycle, many caregivers turn to sleep medications. Unfortunately, studies show that most sleeping pills buy people only an extra twelve to twenty minutes of sleep, at most, per night—and if they are more effective than that, they don't necessarily produce long-term results. Then there are the unpleasant side effects that many experience from taking sleep medications. Some popular sleep medicines even interfere with REM cycles, thus suppressing dreams and the memory-boosting effects of restorative sleep. Like I said, it's a vicious cycle.

There is some good news, however. There is a healthy and holistic approach to sleep that can help caregivers. Taking a more mindful approach to sleep and creating good bedtime habits have been proven to be effective for getting more and better rest.

I offer the following tips (and others throughout this booklet) knowing full well from first-hand experience that it may not be possible to incorporate all of these suggestions at once. Try one at a time and see which ones work for you. Keep an open mind and be gentle with yourself.

- Schedule time for sleep. This can be the most difficult step of all, especially for caregivers whose schedules become so packed that we can barely squeeze in time to eat well, let alone to get enough sleep. But this is also the most important step, so it is worth reviewing your day to see how you can make a commitment to get into bed at a reasonable hour.

- Meditate in the evening. Create a cozy corner using cushions and candles—or whatever gives you comfort—where you can relax and get quiet. Spend five minutes or more sometime between dinner and bedtime to settle the mind. Choose a serene focus, such as filling your heart with love, to soothe the nervous system and get ready to rest.

- Prepare the body for sleep with a few stretches or yoga poses. This helps move your attention from your head, where stressful thoughts can hijack your attempts at sleep, anchoring it instead in your body so you can settle into stillness.

- Count your blessings, rather than counting sheep. Studies have shown that people who go to bed grateful sleep and dream better. Think of small moments of pleasure. A hot cup of tea or a smile from a clerk at the store are reason enough to be grateful.

- Take a deep breath. Slowing the breath can help quiet your thoughts. A simple breath retention practice, like the "4-7-8 Breath"—a breathing pattern recommended by Dr. Andrew Weil that's based on a yogic technique—can help any time of day, but especially when you need to sleep. To do it, inhale for four breaths, gently retain for seven, and exhale for eight. Repeat the process several times until you feel calmer.

- Don't watch the clock. Checking the time when you wake in the middle of the night generally adds to sleep-stealing stress. Instead, accept the fact that you can't necessarily control the number of hours you sleep, and focus on a positive affirmation such as "I am relaxed," syncing the words with your breath.

Tzivia Gover

The Case of the Missing Bedsheets

Looking back I can't help marvel at the symbolism in the fact that this story begins with bedsheets. After all, I'm a dreamworker, and bedsheets offer the perfect symbol for a story about dreams. But at the time, when I was just starting to face the fact that my mother's memory loss was more than just a byproduct of normal aging, the situation was no mere metaphor. I was suffering, and my pain felt concrete—as in hard, cold, and impenetrable.

On this day, I had traveled from my home in Massachusetts to my mother's in Manhattan as I'd done so many times before. But now the visits weren't just occasions for us to catch up, shop, eat, and see a movie. Now, I was checking up on her, too, because each time I visited I was finding more evidence that her memory was challenged and her thinking was muddled.

Even still, we had our routine: When I arrived she'd have treats from the neighborhood bakery arrayed on a plate, and when I climbed the stairs to the guest room, she'd have already made up the sofa bed for me. But recently, things had begun to change. The pastries might still be sitting in a paper bag on the counter, and she'd wait until I got there so we could make the bed together.

On this visit there were no baked treats, the bed was still folded into the couch, and when I went to make it up I couldn't find the sheets or pillowcases anywhere. I asked my mother what had happened to them, but she said she didn't know. I searched the shelves and hamper. No sheets. Maybe she'd forgotten them at the laundry down the street, as she was now forgetting appointments, what she'd gone to the corner deli for, and even the word for thumb. Whatever had happened to the linens would remain a mystery. It was late, I was tired, and there was no choice but to sleep on the bare mattress.

I wanted to burst into tears, as I would have done decades ago as a cranky toddler in this same woman's presence. Instead, I looked at my mother's helpless expression, assured her it was fine, and tried to sleep. I knew that with the disappearance of the sheets, any possibility that my beautiful, intelligent, cultured mother might ever take care of me again, was gone, too.

I would have to wake up to the fact that my mother was losing her mind to dementia, and would likely die of Alzheimer's. Unable to take all that in just yet, I instead cried into the naked pillow over the missing sheets.

Forgotten Dreams

The next morning, I woke with a dream that was as bare as that bed. All I recalled was a voice: "Nothing matters," it said.

Usually fluent in the language of my dreams, I couldn't make sense of this one. What was the dream telling me? That having no clean sheets doesn't matter? That my mother's brain dying, meaning that she was dying, doesn't matter? The fact that I had not yet finished being cared for by her, and now I had to be the caregiver—was the dream saying that none of it mattered?

It would be easy to dispute any of those messages. But the message from the dream bypassed logic. Far from sounding cruel or nihilistic to me, the words landed like a sudden sun shower, leaving me calm and oddly comforted.

Nothing matters.

I could see the truth of the statement, even while its opposite was also true: Life's quotidian details *do* matter. But now I could simultaneously access a perspective from which life's day-to-day disappointments—and even gut-wrenching losses—are but pebbles on a road that is much wider and leads to something much greater than we can imagine.

Through the years of my mother's illness, this dream message continued to resonate within me and reveal its truth. The things I thought were important—whether my mother remembered my birthday or my name, the names of things in general, the layers of her identity that slipped away one-by-one (educator, educated, feminist, mother)—all mattered terribly, and they didn't matter at all.

What's eternal—love, empathy, healing, joy—is what really matters.

Turns out it was never about the sheets or having a mother who made the bed for me. It was something else that truly mattered.

Waking Up When Sleep Is Scarce

Sometimes no matter what you try, you just can't sleep. Here are some techniques to help you feel restored and refreshed on those days when you just can't coax (or strong-arm) sleep into gracing you with a nice long visit.

- Deep, conscious, breathing lowers stress and boosts energy. Try focusing on slowing and lengthening your breath so it fills your low belly (below the navel) on every inhale. Exhale completely, as if you are squeezing the last drop out of a toothpaste tube, as you gently draw in your lower abdomen and navel to empty the last bit of air. Take ten slow breaths like this a few times a day.

- Try yoga nidra. Better than a power nap, yoga nidra is a meditation that can take about twenty minutes or less, and can make you feel rested, almost as if you've had a full night's sleep. I recommend finding a guided yoga nidra CD by Jennifer Reis or another teacher trained in the technique. Or, just find instructions on the internet.

- Don't worry yourself into exhaustion. Rather than dwell on difficulties, fret over the future, or ruminate about the past, try this: Focus on the colors, sounds, or textures around you. Start by focusing on what you see around you, noting colors, shapes, and so on. Then move to what you can hear, feel, smell, etc. Anytime a thought pops up, return your focus to your five senses.

- Even a bad night's sleep has some benefits. Interrupted sleep can sometimes help with dream recall. That's because awakenings during the night often happen at the end of a REM cycle, which is the perfect time to catch a dream!

"The willingness to show up changes us, It makes us a little braver each time."

— Brené Brown

A Conversation in Dreams

While clearing out my mother's closets in preparation for moving her to a memory care facility, I found some of her diaries. Sitting amongst piles of her spiral notebooks, yellow legal pads, and hard-backed journals, I quickly noticed how often she recorded dreams, sometimes more than one each day, in vivid detail.

I wondered how it was possible that in our countless hours of conversation, over meals and cups of herbal tea, while taking long walks through city parks, she had never told me she was such a prolific dreamer. I felt how sad it was that now that I knew, it was too late for us to discuss this gift that we shared in common.

Then again, I never used to tell most people that I remember several dreams each morning. I assumed that everybody did. But when I finally had the opportunity to delve into my lifelong fascination with dreams, I learned that although everybody dreams several times each night, most people remember only one or two a week. Clearly my mother and I were outliers in that regard.

As it happens, it was right around the time that I began to study dreams in earnest that my mother began to slip into dementia, which in her case included aphasia, a language disorder that stripped her of coherent speech. So we hadn't had the chance to compare notes about our dream lives—and now it was too late.

I packed her diaries into a carton and marched downstairs to where she sat slumped on the sofa. I looked directly into her cloudy eyes and asked, "Mom, when were you going to tell me that you are a dreamer, too?"

She gave me a mute grin, which could have meant anything. Nonetheless, I continued–picking up her hand, and softening my voice. "I understand that we can't talk the way we used to, but you can come and visit in my dreams, and we can talk there," I said.

The next night I dreamed the phone was ringing, and when I picked it up I heard her voice. We talked and laughed. I asked her how she's doing, and she told me what was challenging about having Alzheimer's. Then she said, "It's not great. But it's not too terrible either."

Call it what you like: The Power of Suggestion. Wish Fulfillment. Coincidence. The fact is that from that day forward, and even now, years after her death, she has continued to call or visit from time to time in my dreams.

Tzivia Gover

Caregivers Need Care, Too: And Dreams Can Help

Normally when I was facing a tough time I'd pick up the phone and call my mother. But in this case, when my stress as a caregiver was rising, the person who in the past would have advised me, sent me notes of encouragement and gifts to brighten my day could no longer do any of that.

Again, I was not alone in my frustration and loss. The caregiver of someone with dementia or Alzheimer's is often the child, spouse, or other loved one who once counted on this person for support. When that person can no longer function in the same way, the caregiver must look to other sources of care and comfort. In these times of great loss it feels like there is nothing that can completely take away the pain and sense of isolation. But my dreams remind me again and again that we all have an internal support system that we can tap into day or night.

What follows are ways caregivers can use their dreams for help and sustenance.

- Keep a journal. Write about what you are going through during the day as well as the dreams you have at night. Include details and descriptions, using as many of your five senses as you can. Take your time and allow insights and new awarenesses to arise without pushing for them.

- Share dreams with a friend or therapist. If people are unsure how to respond to your dreams, assure them you don't expect them to interpret your dream. Simple questions like, "How did the dream make you feel?" or "What does that dream make you think about?" are often all we need to connect with our inner wisdom and with one another.

- Ask other caregivers about their dreams. Talking to other caregivers, paid or unpaid, about their dreams is a good way to encourage meaningful connection. Also, ask the person with dementia about their dreams for as long you're able to carry on conversations. This is a great way to invite authentic conversations and feel close to one another in what can be a difficult time.

- Make time for reflection. When you are a caregiver there's little time to attend to yourself and your own needs, let alone do dreamwork. But you can reflect on your dreams during long waits in doctors' offices, or while commuting on planes or trains to care for your loved one. Even when you're too tired to take a bath or read a book you can close your eyes and think about a dream you've had.

Tzivia Gover

Solace on the Page

Keeping a Journal for Dreams and Waking

One caregiver I spoke with described the loneliness she experienced when her husband could no longer communicate because of dementia. Without her beloved companion to process her day, she felt adrift. So, she began talking to herself—on the pages of a notebook that became her journal.

Journaling helps relieve stress and supports mental and physical health and well-being. In addition, studies now show that describing your experiences and feelings in a journal improves memory and may even help to prevent Alzheimer's disease.

Journaling your dreams has also been shown to be beneficial for memory and Alzheimer's prevention. Although I haven't found the research to explain why this is, I have my own theory. When we dream, different parts of our brain are activated that are "offline" when we're awake, and vice versa. Notably, the language centers that are responsible for writing are less active when dreaming, as is short-term memory. So by writing dreams we are helping to balance our brains as we bring writing and memory together with our nighttime dreams.

In addition, writing dreams also helps with dream recall, so you'll have more access to the creative, problem-solving, and healing potential of your dreams.

Here are some tips to help you get started.

- Choose a book. Whether it be a simple spiral-bound notebook or fancy blank book, keep your journal by your bedside. Before you turn out the lights, write about the highlights of your day. In addition to other benefits, this practice helps clear your mind so you can sleep and dream better.

- Take a moment to remember. Before you move or speak in the morning, reflect on your dreams. There's no need to analyze or even understand them; simply review them as you would look back on an eventful day. Scan them for any information that might give you a new perspective — that might startle, amuse, entertain, or inform you.

- Write your dreams. Do this first thing in the morning. You may think you'll remember your dreams later in the day, but for most people dream recall fades quickly.

Forgotten Dreams

"Yea, all things live forever, though at times they sleep and are forgotten."

— H. Rider Haggard, *She: A History of Adventure*

A Waking Nightmare

It started slowly, as these things so often do.

My mother would call me up, and we'd enjoy a nice talk.

Ten minutes later she'd call again, as if our conversation had never happened.

If I pointed out what just happened, she'd sometimes deny it. Other times, she'd admit to her lapses, as if she were admitting to having shoplifted a lipstick from the Duane Reade pharmacy down the street.

As the months passed, the memory slips grew in frequency and intensity. She'd confide in me that she'd taken the subway to a restaurant downtown to meet a friend, but when the train doors opened, she couldn't remember why she was there, so she turned back and went home. Shaken and embarrassed, she'd beg me not to tell anyone.

I encouraged her to see her doctor and get help. But her mounting fears kept her from looking into the situation. I told her, as I used to tell my daughter during her teen years when she tried to hide troubles she faced in school or with a friend: "Problems grow in the dark. When we shine light on them, they tend to shrink back to a manageable size."

But my mother couldn't bear to shine light on what was happening. She employed evasion and white lies to cover over her lapses. She would feign a coughing fit to stall for time when she couldn't remember a common word or phrase, and laughed off "slips of the tongue" as if she found them amusing.

As a professional dreamworker I recognize this tendency to try to run from scary things. In my line of work I see that people resist talking about bad dreams and nightmares, as if putting words to them will give them more power. But the opposite is true: When we turn toward the monster and look it in the eye, we assess our opponent as well as our resources for dealing with it. With dream villains, we can use our imagination to ask questions and get the information we need, or we can call on superpowers to overcome the situation. Awake, we can fight our fears with knowledge, and start to search out creative or straight-forward solutions.

Alzheimer's can feel like a bogeyman—a sinister intruder lurking in the corners making the healthiest among us shudder with fear at each forgotten word or name, or the realization that we've put the half-

and-half in the tea cupboard instead of the refrigerator.

Researching the facts of the situation, talking to friends about our uneasiness, and getting checked out by a medical professional are good ways to take a more constructive approach.

Here are some tips for people who are worried about memory issues of their own or their loved ones.

- Light up the darkness. In the face of a diagnosis of dementia or Alzheimer's, whether for yourself or a loved one, illuminate the situation with information and knowledge. To get started, contact the Alzheimer's Association or other reputable organizations and get accurate, research-based information.

- Choose love over fear. In dreamwork we learn that when we face a terrifying antagonist, if we call on divine love, the scenario will shift, and a peaceful solution will be reached. To begin to bring the light of love to the situation you are facing in waking life (or in a dream), try repeating the phrase,

  "I choose love," as a mantra or affirmation. Then look for ways to respond to your fears or worries with a loving heart, showering kindness and compassion on yourself, your loved ones, and the situation as a whole.

- Superpowers aren't just for comic book characters. In the world of dreams and imagination we can discover our super powers when we face a nightmare scenario. Likewise, life's challenges and waking nightmares help us discover our own everyday super powers. What strengths have you developed—or might you—from your experience as a caregiver? Perhaps your super power is positive thinking, compassion, serenity, or bringing joy to yourself and others through baking special treats, singing or playing music, or humor. Perhaps you have great research skills or organizational abilities. Some people have the super power of networking to find professionals and other helpers for themselves and their loved ones. Brainstorm on a piece of paper to discover your superpowers, or ask someone who loves you to help you identify yours.

Shaken Awake: What to do when you wake from a nightmare

Waking from a nightmare is scary and disorienting. Often all we want to do is forget the disturbing dream. But it's important to take care of yourself, and to remember that nightmares come to us, as I believe all dreams do, in the service of health, help, and healing. Here are some suggestions for how to respond when you've had a scary or disturbing dream.

- Bring yourself home. Sit up in bed and remind yourself that you're safe now. Look around the room and name what you see, including the color: "There's my white bedspread, there is the red loveseat, there are the yellow curtains," etc. This simple exercise helps calm you and bring your attention back to the present moment. Then get out of bed and get a drink of water to soothe yourself, and complete the transition out of the dream and back into your body.

- Pick up your pen. It's understandable to want to forget a nightmare, but nightmares are your dreaming mind's way to get your attention to help you face a difficult emotional situation. You can't get the healing from the dream unless you remember it. So, write it down as soon as possible, and share it with a trusted friend or therapist when you are ready.

- Spin it. A spin doctor finds a positive angle on a potentially damaging story or event. While this is often done to cover or avoid the truth, in healthy dreamwork we practice an authentic and productive version of spinning events: Look at the dream from different angles. For example, if you have a dream that you are being chased, ask yourself what is pursuing you in waking life. The answer might be an emotion you're avoiding, or a tense situation you are ignoring. If there's a frightening animal, like a bear clawing at your door to get inside, try to find out what the threatening animal wants or needs. Is there a way you could use that bear's ferocity to help you, rather than hurt you? Keep spinning the dream elements until you find their healing or helpful qualities.

Dreamwork for the Worried Well

The "worried well" are those of us who are healthy—but anxious about the possibility that we might one day experience dementia or Alzheimer's.

For example, I have a family history of dementia—and also of anxiety. So worry and fear exaggerate my concerns about my brain health.

To calm my fears I've asked my dreams what I can do to improve my cognitive well-being. Some of the information I received I might as easily have learned from doing some research online or asking my doctor. But when I learn it in a dream the knowledge gets my attention in a way words from a website or health professional don't.

For example, repeatedly being told by health care professionals that sugar is compromising my mental and physical health hadn't motivated me to give up my fondness for cakes, muffins, and cookies in the way that a single dream did. In the years since having my "no-sugar" dream, I've cut back my consumption so that now I only have a sugary dessert once a month or so. My motivation was strengthened when I learned that eating sugar contributes having a high glycemic index, which research now shows is bad for brain health and might contribute to Alzheimer's.

Most people think dreams are random occurrences over which we have no control. But with even a little effort and practice, most anyone can incubate a dream. In addition to providing helpful information, setting dream intentions makes us more conscious agents of our lives, both asleep and awake. Here's how to get started.

- Practice remembering your dreams by taking an interest in them. Write them down, draw them, and/or record them using the voice memos feature on your phone. Even if you don't remember a dream, record anything at all you do remember, including emotions, a felt sense of having dreamt about a general situation or topic, etc.

- Once you can reliably remember your dreams, you're ready to try to incubate the answer to a specific question. Before bed set an intention: "Tonight in my dreams I will learn about …" "Tonight in my dreams I will see what's in store if I decide to …" "Tonight in my dreams I'll find healing for …" Don't ask "Yes or No" questions; dreams are better at responding to open-ended questions and exploring possibilities.

Forgotten Dreams

- To help you focus on your question, put a picture or object that represents your intention near your bed, or under your pillow or mattress.

- Record your dream in the morning and review it for ways it might connect with your intention. If you don't remember any dreams, try again until you do.

- Expect results! Have faith that whatever dream you receive is the answer to your question, even if you don't see the connection right away. Consult a dream therapist or an interested friend to explore the dream and find where it connects to your query.

Tzivia Gover

Storm Clouds Gather

At the end of what felt like the worst day of several years' worth of worsening days while my mom lived with Alzheimer's, I walked the seventy-four blocks and three avenues from her New York City apartment to my stepmother's apartment downtown to spend the night.

I needed that time to walk off (as if I could) the sadness, anger, and heartbreak of watching my mother crying in pain, unable to tell me or her paid caregiver what was the matter, due to the aphasia that had taken her ability to speak coherently. I didn't feel like I could face another day of this nightmare. But when I closed my eyes that night, another nightmare began to unfold.

I dreamed I was on an island where a storm was brewing. I rushed to the airport to get a flight out, but was told no planes were leaving until the storm was over. I had no choice but to find what safety I could on that not-so-dreamy island. There were no houses or buildings to take refuge in, so I scrambled to high ground and stood among the wind-whipped palm trees. I watched in fear as ocean waves crested as high as the skyscrapers that lined the horizon in my mother's neighborhood.

You don't need to be a dream expert to recognize the symbolism in that one. Its imagery captured how trapped and helpless I felt as I faced the tempest of my mother's disease.

But then in the dream, the winds subsided and the waves calmed. I headed down the hill to the sea to find people frolicking in the friendly surf—as if that same sea hadn't terrorized us hours before. After only a moment's hesitation, I waded into the water and joined them.

I woke from the dream, not only refreshed by the sense of playful immersion in the sea—but also ready to face the day.

Those island denizens of my dream reminded me that life is full of nightmare winds, but also blissful play. The world wasn't betraying my mother or me by visiting this unwanted disease on our family. Storms come and go, and affect anyone in their path. If you can't escape the tempest, you do your best to withstand it. Alzheimer's was a storm we would weather, and there would surely be happiness again.

That tropical breeze of hope was all I needed just then. It might as easily have come from the consoling words of a loved one, but coming in the form of a dream the message washed through me at a cellular level, and washed away my tears, so I could face another day.

Forgotten Dreams

As if conjured by the dream, that morning, as I
turned down my mother's street, I saw my daughter
waiting on the stoop for me with a bouquet of
sunflowers. It was a surprise visit, as unexpected
as a blue-bright day after the storm has passed.

Tzivia Gover

Something You Love

I was lucky. Caring for my mother meant spending time with her in a city I love that is filled with happy memories of enjoying parks, museums and cafes together. But once she got sick, I barely left her apartment during my visits, except to run errands or slowly walk with her up and down the block. I soon realized that if I were to survive the marathon of caregiving I'd have to take breaks.

I committed to doing something I loved every time I went to New York. Sometimes that meant taking a brief detour to sit in a playground and watch children careen down the slide on my way to or from an errand. Sometimes I stopped into a museum or gallery for even an hour before or after arriving at my mother's apartment. Touching in with beauty sparks pleasure in one's heart in an instant. Bringing a bouquet of flowers to my mother so we both could enjoy them was another way I could connect with something I loved—and share it with her.

Try to do something you love every day—especially during times of stress. A five-minute evening walk, or a glance out the window to admire the stars and moon, sketching with colored pencils or putting on a favorite song and listening with your eyes closed …anything will do.

Acknowledge the fact that you treated yourself in this way. Make note of the experience in your journal, tell a loved one what you did, or replay the event your mind as you fall asleep. Savor the good feelings and amplify them in your mind.

"Our birth is but a sleep and a forgetting."

— William Wordsworth, *The Major Works*

Dreaming into the Twilight Zone

In a Time of Grief, Dreams Point the Way to Joy

After years of helping to care for my mother and witnessing the ravages of a disease that stripped her of memory, identity, and language, I was eager to learn more about joy, which at times during my grieving process felt as if it existed on a distant planet–not at the center of my five-foot, four-inch body. And yet, that was just what my yoga teacher promised. During a yoga retreat I learned that there is a bliss body that resides at the center of our being, no matter what is going on or how we are perceiving our experience.

I wasn't feeling particularly blissful during those final months of my mother's illness, or during my grieving process after she died. So, I attended a lecture about the five subtle bodies, or koshas as they are called in yogic teachings, in order to learn more. According to this system of belief, our physical body is just one layer that makes up who we are. We also contain, sheathed one inside the other, the energy body, the psycho-emotional body, the wisdom body, and at the center of them all, the joy or bliss body.

After the lecture my mind was swimming with new information, as well as curiosity and some doubts about whether there was any truth to these concepts. So, when I went to sleep, I asked my dreams to show me how to locate that inner body of joy or bliss. Here's what happened:

In my dream I found myself in a dark, freezing cold house, filled with sleeping people in all of the rooms. As I walked through the corridors and peeked through doorways, I encountered one of my favorite sitcom characters, Rory from "Gilmore Girls." In this episode (no spoiler-alert needed, this dream has gone off-script) Rory is mourning the death of her mother. Even in the dream I was aware that Rory's relationship with her mom, with whom she has a very close friendship, was similar to my relationship with my mother, and that her grief mirrored my own.

I woke briefly in the middle of the night, thinking how far off the dream was from answering my question; there was no joy in it, after all. But then I realized the sleeping bodies in a near-freezing house might represent the "subtle bodies" within myself that were stuck in icy cold grief and keeping me from experiencing bliss.

Forgotten Dreams

So I reset my intention to experience my joy body and went back to sleep.

This time in my dream I was walking down a hallway when I heard a phone ringing. I turned to answer it, and when I picked up the receiver I heard my mother's voice, as clear and bright as if she were standing beside me. I called out for my siblings to come listen in.

"I have something great to tell you guys, you're going to love this!" my mother said.

My siblings and I were filled with glee. Whatever she wanted to tell us seemed beside the point. The wonder was that she was there at all, talking and laughing like her old self.

It had been years since we'd heard that happy, easy voice. The voice that seemed to have a smile curled into its syllables, a little twist of irony around the edges, and a hint of Brooklyn in its dropped t's (bo-uhl for bottle) and squawking vowels (caw-fee for coffee).

Then, just before I was about to wake up, and thus "hang up" the call, my mother announced that she was with "the guy from 'The Twilight Zone.'" My siblings and I burst into a new bout of laughter, imagining Mom with a seemingly random, retro TV character.

And then I woke back in the world without her.

I was buoyed for a time by the pure joy of our dream visit. Then I began to reflect on what else the dream might have been telling me about where to find the joy body, and how to access it.

The dream reminded me that despite my mother's physical death, there is an eternal connection between my mother, my siblings and me. My mother was just a phone call away.

But this wasn't really news. After all, how many times had people, in an effort to comfort me, repeated that my mother would always be with me in spirit, that love never dies—and all of the other clichéd condolences of Hallmark cards and well-meaning friends. Those sentiments alone are powerless against the tidal waves of grief that come with mourning. The dream, however, allowed me to experience the truth behind those hackneyed phrases and canned words. That felt experience that came through the dream was truly comforting.

And there was more: The dream led me deeper into the twilight zone. It was inviting me into the fifth dimension. It turns out that when my mother said she was with "the guy from 'The Twilight Zone,'" she was offering some enlightening information cloaked in the garb of a cheesy TV show.

Growing up, I watched reruns of "The Twilight Zone," but I was too young to have really gotten into the series, which aired from 1959 to 1965. So after I had the dream I went online to remember who "the guy" from the show was, and to see what connection he might have to my question about the joy body. My Google search led me to Rod Serling, the show's creator, and these words from the show's introduction as it was voiced in Season One:

There is a fifth dimension beyond that which is known to man. It is a dimension as vast as space and as timeless as infinity. It is the middle ground between light and shadow, between science and superstition, and it lies between the pit of man's fears and the summit of his knowledge. This is the dimension of imagination. It is an area which we call the Twilight Zone.

Sitting in front of my laptop's screen, I had to blink my eyes to be sure I wasn't still dreaming. That description, I now saw, was like a guide to the bliss body and where to find it. It could indeed be described as a vast, infinite, timeless dimension between shadow and light, beyond fear and on the path to true knowledge or enlightenment.

In grieving over my mother's disease and death, I had to move through my inner shadows and fears to find the joy that still lived at the center of my being. I had to look beyond what I could see awake, to the timeless dimension of dreams and imagination to truly experience it.

This experience reminded me once more that dreams don't just "happen *to* us." They are a nightly journey into a twilight zone that we can traverse skillfully. Each morning we return from our exploration of the fifth dimension where we can gather wisdom and comfort to soothe our fears and help us move through grief—and into joy.

It's Not 'Just' a Dream

We say it's "just" a dream, or "just" your imagination. But that little word *just* points to a big problem. Our imagination, including our dreaming mind, is a powerful tool for visualization, which can help empower real change. Leading with the word "just" diminishes the power of our inner worlds. Instead, drop the word "just" and honor these inner riches that can help you gain and maintain health and healing.

When we combine a dream image with strong positive emotions, and meditate briefly on them, we support our body and mind's efforts toward health and healing.

One way to empower this process is to incubate dreams: Before bed, introduce a suggestion into your subconscious by asking your dreams how you can help yourself or a loved one. Whether you recall your dreams or not, setting this suggestion before sleep when the body is already primed to heal itself, supercharges the naturally therapeutic potential for sleep and dreams.

You can use this same technique in a guided meditation when awake. Use your imagination to see in vivid detail what health looks like to you, and let yourself feel the strong favorable emotions associated with being vibrant, healthy and happy. Studies show that our minds can have a positive and powerful effect on our bodies.

Tzivia Gover

"No one tires of dreaming, because to dream is to forget, and forgetting does not weigh on us, it is a dreamless sleep throughout which we remain awake. In dreams I have achieved everything."

— Fernando Pessoa, *The Book of Disquiet*

Rats from Heaven

As I stood on the platform waiting for the uptown Q train on a Saturday afternoon in August, I couldn't help but think about my mother. That's not the least bit unusual. My mother, who had died about a year and a half before, loved everything about "her" city, from the Metropolitan, to the Bowery, from the corner deli where she bought her daily copy of the New York Times and bouquets of flowers to the finest restaurants—and from the city's soaring architecture to the lawns of Central Park. She even loved the subway on a sweltering summer afternoon.

I remembered how, when we stood on the subway platform together, my mom would always look toward the direction the train would be coming from, and watch for the first glimpse of light that would signal that a train was approaching. When she said she loved watching for that tiny glimmer of light in the dark tunnel, it was as if she were imparting to me her philosophy of life. She once told me she was a closet optimist; that despite her frequent and vocal worries, neuroses, and anxieties, that deep down, she secretly expected the best. Each time we waited for the subway together we practiced the art of looking for the coming of the light.

Another thing I remembered was how my beautiful, stylish, cultured, and elegant mother loved to look into the cavern of the subway tracks, and peer into the little caves made by the platform overhangs. Turns out, she was searching for rats. Over time, we made a game—no, a competition—of it. As we waited for the train that would take us to a museum or the botanical gardens or a favorite store, we'd look for rats in the tracks, and whichever one of us saw one first would shout it out and we would get a strange rush of glee.

So as I waited for the Q train that day, I sent a little hello up to my mom in heaven, and asked her to let me see a rat. Instead, I looked to my left and saw the subway's light sweeping the walls of the tunnel, and then the train thundered into the station, and I got onboard. I was headed uptown where I'd meet my brother for a cup of iced coffee, then dinner with my daughter and a Broadway show.

After the show, a cool breeze was blowing so I decided to walk downtown rather than take the subway. As I crossed Union Square, just before

Forgotten Dreams

midnight, something scurried across my path, not six inches from my sandaled feet. I'd been on the phone with my then-fiance, who was back home in Massachusetts, when I squealed: "A mouse just ran right in front of me!"

"Sweetie, you're in New York City, are you sure it wasn't a rat?" he asked. Well, I conceded it was pretty big for a mouse. Two women sitting on a bench nearby, who'd seen me jump and overheard my conversation, nodded in affirmation: It was a rat.

I forgave myself for not identifying the rodent for what it was. After all, other than the ones I'd seen in the subway with my mother, which were at a safe distance several feet below where we stood on the platform, I hadn't encountered a rat in decades.

But in all the excitement of the day, and in the hours that had transpired since my subway ride that afternoon, I'd forgotten all about my prayer to my mother. It wasn't until I was tucked into bed an hour or so later that I realized the rat that almost tickled my toes as it scooted past must have been my mother's doing. She'd sent that rat to me, as her way of winking down from heaven.

At least, that's what I choose to believe—the same way my mother chose to believe in the hope heralded by the light of a train, and which stood in for her secret store of optimism. Or maybe it's just my way of finding beauty in the unlikeliest of places—even in her eventual disease and death. Just like my mother did throughout her life, when

she insisted on loving every inch of her city, rats
and all.

Dreaming Together

When juggling child care, relationships, caregiving for a parent or spouse, work, and more, the key is to not go it alone. Instead, create a good team.

A successful team pulls together for one goal, and a good coach brings out the best in a team by identifying and encouraging individual strengths to create a winning whole. A team also needs motivation to help its members keep striving toward their goal, even when spirits are flagging.

For me, contacting the Alzheimer's Association and signing up with my siblings to participate in the annual Alzheimer's walk was one way to bring together our team of paid and unpaid caregivers, along with family members and friends who wanted to be supportive but didn't quite know what to do. For several years, during my mother's illness and now after her death, we have united as "Team Loving Jane" for the walk. Each year we have enjoyed the warmth of being surrounded by others who knew the same struggles we faced. Some years there have even been cheerleaders dressed in the purple and white Alzheimer's Association colors waving pom poms along the route. Afterward we all go out for a celebratory lunch.

In the process of preparing for the walk and collecting pledges in dollar amounts from the single digits into the hundreds from co-workers, friends, and family, we also receive words of support and comfort. Best of all, perhaps, each year we come together to share quality time as family and friends, engaged in an activity filled with meaning and hope—even in the face of a heartbreaking disease.

Have you created your team? Think about it: You likely already have some friends and professionals you can turn to for help. These are your team members.Here are some thoughts on bringing your team together, so you don't have to go it alone.

- Who's on your team? List the names of family and friends, medical professionals, social workers, and others who have in any way supported you and your loved ones on this journey. In my case, when I felt sorry for myself and my mom, I'd make lists of all the people on our team who did sweet things for us: Patty invited my brother and me over for home-cooked meals. My aunt and uncle joined us for the Alzheimer's walk. My sister cajoled me into being playful and dancing in the living room with Mom, even on our worst days. My brother always nurtured our hearts, saying "I love you" every time he texted, called, greeted us or said goodbye. My dad, who was divorced from my mom for decades, called often to see how I was doing, and acted as referee on the rare occasions when my siblings and I would quarrel, or when I got frustrated with another family member or paid caregiver. Naming our team members and their special skills and contributions helped me keep self-pity at bay, instead feeding my sense of comfort and community.

- How do you encourage members of your team? Encouragement comes in packages small and large: A sincere thank-you acknowledging what you appreciate about a team member can make a world of difference. My sister and brother had a knack for doing special things for our paid caregivers, such as bringing them little gifts, writing them thank-you notes, or taking them out for a meal.

- What would be your team's mascot? Think of what animal embodies the strengths your team has or needs. You can even watch your dreams to see if a particular animal shows up. You might choose an animal like the eagle, whose "eagle eye" can offer a combination of perspective and focus; or the lion, who is famous for its ferocity in protecting its family, and also for its heart and courage. Early in my mother's Alzheimer's journey, I had a dream about a dog that helped to remind me to pause to give and receive affection and appreciate the bond of loyalty and companionship that I shared with my mother.

- Use social media to keep connected. My family and friends created a "Loving Jane" private Facebook page where we offered updates on my mother's health and requests for support. It also became a forum to extend encouragement to one another. There are other online platforms designed specifically for keeping friends and family connected online as well. A Google search for "online resources for caregivers" will get you started.

Acknowledgments

My Dream Team

Caring for a loved one with Alzheimer's or dementia is a team effort. So too is writing. My own healing journey as well as the process of writing this booklet has been supported and enhanced by my family, friends and colleagues.

I owe special thanks to The Alzheimer's Association of New York City and Long Island, my mother's paid caregivers including Grace, Iris, Noumou and Torbari.

I also want to thank my family of dreamers at the International Association for the Study of Dreams (IASD) and beyond who provided information, friendship, and spiritual sustenance for me on this journey, especially Justina Lasley, Sherry Treadaway Puricelli, and many others.

Thank you to Suzanne Wilson for sharing her editing talents with me, and to the members of the Writing Room at Forbes Library for listening to and commenting on drafts of the pieces that make up this book.

Bouquets of sunflowers go also to my loving family and family of friends including my brother, James Gover, who cared for my mother with unmatched devotion and love, my husband Lou, and my daughter Miranda. My sister, father, and stepmother, my aunt and uncle, were also among the MVPs on "Team Loving Jane."

Versions of many of these pieces and more information on dreams and caregiving can be found at: http://tziviagover.com/blog/

Resources

- The Alzheimer's Association. Formed in 1980, the Alzheimer's Association is the leading voluntary health organization in Alzheimer's care, support and research. https://www.alz.org/

- The International Association for the Study of Dreams. IASD is a non-profit, international, multidisciplinary organization dedicated to the pure and applied investigation of dreams and dreaming. http://iasdreams.org/

- The Institute for Dream Studies. IDS provides educational and training opportunities in dreams, dreamwork and dream group leadership through lectures, workshops, and its Dream Certification Program. http://institutefordreamstudies.org/

Tzivia Gover

About the Author

Tzivia Gover is the author of *The Mindful Way to a Good Night's Sleep*, *Joy in Every Moment,* and *Learning in Mrs. Towne's House.* She is a writer, educator, and certified dream therapist and the director of the Institute of Dream Studies. Gover has led numerous workshops and panels about dreams, mindfulness, and writing, and she holds an MFA in writing from Columbia University. She is an active member of the International Association for the Study of Dreams and the founder of 350 Dreamers, an international network of people who dream together for global healing. She lives in Northampton, Massachusetts, and can be found online at tziviagover.com.

Photo credit Ann Chwatsky. The author and her mother, circa 1995.

Tzivia Gover

Forgotten Dreams

The Mindful Way to a Good Night's Sleep

This accessible guide to cultivating deep, restful sleep — naturally — combines author Tzivia Gover's expertise in both mindfulness and dreamwork. Along with a healthy dose of encouragement, Gover offers practical lifestyle advice, simple yoga poses, 10-minute meditations, and easy breathing exercises, plus visualization and journaling activities. You'll also learn how to set the scene for safe, productive dreaming and cultivate your dream recall. This holistic approach extends into your waking hours with tips on morning routines to ensure that sound sleep leads to refreshed, more conscious living all day long.

Made in the USA
Lexington, KY
07 December 2019